SOLOS
for the
CELLO
PLAYER

With Piano Accompaniment

Selected and Edited by

OTTO DERI

On the accompaniment recordings:

STEFANIE JACOB, JUDIT JAIMES and
JEANNIE YU

pianists

To access companion recorded piano accompaniments online, visit:
www.halleonard.com/mylibrary

"Enter Code"
4839-8143-4093-9260

ED 2313-B

ISBN 978-1-61780-611-7

G. SCHIRMER, Inc.

DISTRIBUTED BY

HAL•LEONARD®

Visit Hal Leonard Online at
www.halleonard.com

Contact us:
Hal Leonard
7777 West Bluemound Road
Milwaukee, WI 53213
Email: info@halleonard.com

In Europe, contact:
Hal Leonard Europe Limited
42 Wigmore Street
Marylebone, London, W1U 2RN
Email: info@halleonardeurope.com

In Australia, contact:
Hal Leonard Australia Pty. Ltd.
4 Lentara Court
Cheltenham, Victoria, 3192 Australia
Email: info@halleonard.com.au

PREFACE

The seventeen pieces contained in this volume present material on the intermediate level. The pieces have been selected so that various stylistic periods (Baroque, Classical, Romantic, Impressionistic) are represented. The selections appear in order of difficulty.

Many of the compositions are original cello works. The other selections are adaptations or transcriptions, which should broaden the somewhat limited cello repertory. The fingerings and bowings have been revised by the editor according to the principles of modern cello technique.

CONTENTS

Pianists on the recordings:
[1] Stefanie Jacob
[2] Judit Jaimes
[3] Jeannie Yu

The price of this publication includes access to companion recorded accompaniments online, for download or streaming, using the unique code found on the title page.

Visit **www.halleonard.com/mylibrary** and enter the access code.

1. Lullaby

Transcribed by Otto Deri

Johannes Brahms
(1833–1897)

2. Nina
(Canzonetta)

Giovanni Battista Pergolesi
(1710–1736)

3. Andante
from *Orfeo*

Christoph Willibald Gluck
(1714–1787)

4. La Cinquantaine

(Air in the Olden Style)

Jean Gabriel Marie
(1852–1928)

5. Romance

Claude Debussy
(1862–1918)

6. Larghetto
from Violin Sonata, Op. 1, No. 13

Transcribed by Otto Deri

George Frideric Handel
(1685–1759)

7. Aria

Antonio Lotti
(1666–1740)

8. Lento

from *Five Pieces in Popular Mood*

Robert Schumann
(1810–1856)

9. Bourrée I and II

from Third Cello Suite

Johann Sebastian Bach
(1685–1750)

BOURRÉE I
Poco Allegro

BOURRÉE II

BOURRÉE I

10. Andante

Transcribed by Otto Deri

Ludwig van Beethoven
(1770–1827)

11. The Swan

from *The Carnival of Animals*

Camille Saint-Saëns
(1835–1921)

12. Menuet

from Divertimento in D, K334

Wolfgang Amadeus Mozart
(1756–1791)

13. Sicilienne
Op. 78

Gabriel Fauré
(1845–1924)

14. Allegro
from Violin Sonata, Op. 1, No. 15

Transcribed by Otto Deri

George Frideric Handel
(1685–1759)

15. Village Song
Op. 62, No. 2

David Popper
(1843–1913)

16. Allegro spiritoso

Jean Baptiste Senaillé
(c.1688–1730)

17. Country Dance

Carl Maria von Weber
(1786–1826)

Transcribed by Otto Deri